DEPARTMENT OF THE NAVY
HEADQUARTERS UNITED STATES MARINE CORPS
3000 MARINE CORPS PENTAGON
WASHINGTON, DC 20350-3000

I0430097

MARINE CORPS PARACHUTING POLICY AND PROGRAM ADMINISTRATION

Reports Required: I. Joint Airdrop Summary Report (JASR) (Report Control Symbol EXEMPT), Encl (1), chap. 13, par. 2.a.
II. Annual Airdrop Roster Report (Report Control Symbol EXEMPT), Encl (1), chap 13, par 2.b.
III. Equipment Malfunctions and Incidents Report (Report Control Symbol EXEMPT), Encl (1), chap. 13, par. 3

1. Situation. Individual service parachuting programs are guided by policy directing their conduct and administration by Department of Defense (DOD) executive agents (EA) in accordance with references (a) through (af). Reference (a) assigns the U.S. Army as the EA for all airborne matters common to both the Army and the Marine Corps. This Order establishes policy and procedural guidance for the administration of Marine Corps parachuting programs and takes precedence where Marine Corps equipment and doctrine are not supported by EA policy, procedure and/or doctrine. All Marine Corps parachuting programs will be administered in compliance with this Order.

2. Cancellation. MCO 3500.20B.

3. Mission. The Marine Corps parachuting program supports the development and maintenance of required warfighting capabilities. Policies and procedures described herein are intended to maximize unit and individual combat effectiveness, service interoperability, accountability and safety.

4. Execution

   a. Commander's Intent and Concept of Operations

      (1) Commander's Intent

         (a) All cognizant Commanders and Officers-in-Charge of Marine Corps units performing parachute operations will conduct parachute operations and training in accordance with this Order and other applicable directives. This Order is applicable to both the active and reserve components of the USMC.

         (b) This Order is applicable to all DOD civilian and military personnel assigned to Marine Corps units and activities. When other Service or Component directives conflict with this Order, the Marine Component commander will determine which Order takes precedence.

         (c) This Order establishes the Deputy Commandant for Plans, Policies and Operations (DC, PP&O) as the Marine Corps personnel parachuting proponent and the Deputy Commandant for Installations and Logistics (DC, I&L) as the Marine Corps aerial delivery of cargo proponent.

      (2) Concept of Operations. The Marine Corps develops and maintains static line parachuting, military free fall (MFF) parachuting and air delivery capabilities to meet valid operational requirements, as indicated in CMC-approved unit mission statements and by appropriately coded billets on unit Tables of Organization (T/Os). Details of this policy, to include exceptions, are found in the enclosure to this Order.

b. <u>Subordinate Element Missions</u>

(1) <u>DC, PP&O (POG) shall</u>:

(a) Serve as the USMC proponent, functional expert and supervisor in all matters related to personnel parachuting per enclosure (1) of this Order.

(b) Conduct an annual validation of all parachuting billets and provide applicable Hazardous Duty Incentive Pay (HDIP) budget input to DC, M&RA (MPP) to coincide with budget cycle submissions.

(c) Validate all new parachuting requirements for USMC units and billets as a function of the Total Force Structure process prior to final approval by DC, CD&I.

(d) Prior to initial fielding of new USMC aircraft, coordinate DOD proponent validation and approval of aircraft-specific personnel parachuting procedures.

(2) <u>DC, I&L (LPC) shall</u>:

(a) Serve as the USMC proponent, functional expert and supervisor in all matters related to air delivery per enclosure (1) of this Order.

(b) Participate in the DOD Airdrop Malfunction/Safety Analysis Review Board when requested by Naval Safety Center (NAVSAFECEN).

(c) Serve as the lead USMC representative to the DOD Joint Technical Airdrop Group (JTAG) in accordance with reference (b).

(d) Prior to initial fielding of new USMC aircraft, coordinate DOD proponent validation and approval of aircraft-specific air delivery procedures.

(3) <u>DC, CD&I shall</u>:

(a) In conjunction with DC PP&O (POG), serve as the user representative for all parachuting equipment-related issues, ensuring current parachuting equipment deficiencies are corrected and desired parachuting capabilities support Marine Corps required operational capabilities.

(b) Take all actions necessary to support equipment requirements for parachuting capabilities in compliance with references (c) and (d).

(c) In coordination with Marine Corps Systems Command (MARCORSYSCOM), Infantry Weapons Systems, Raids and Amphibious Reconnaissance (IWS/R), maintain inter-Service liaison to ensure equipment interoperability and facilitate requirement development through appropriate supporting documentation to support parachuting operations.

(d) Participate in all parachute-related Integrated Process Action Teams (IPTs) to identify and resolve logistics issues per chapter 2 of the enclosure to this Order.

(e) Maintain current and future T/Os and Tables of Equipment (T/Es), with mission statements, for all units with valid parachuting requirements.

(f) Maintain current and planned T/E allowances within the Total Force Structure Management System for all units with valid parachuting requirements.

(g) Publish timely updates to any T/O and T/E changes approved to units with valid parachuting requirements.

(4) DC, Aviation shall:

(a) Coordinate DC, PP&O (POG) and DC, I&L (LPC) participation in the development of future aviation capabilities to ensure parachuting requirements are fully considered.

(b) Coordinate DC, PP&O (POG), DC, I&L (LPC), CG, MARCORSYSCOM (IWS/R), and Commander, Naval Safety Center (Code 44) participation in planning for Operational Testing (OT) and Developmental Testing (DT) of aircraft in research, development, test and evaluation (RDT&E) to ensure procedures for personnel parachuting and air delivery are developed, validated and approved by the DOD parachuting proponents prior to aircraft fielding.

(5) CG, Training Command (C461TP) shall:

(a) Conduct an annual validation of all Marine Corps parachuting related formal school requirements via the Training Input Plan (TIP) process per reference (e), and provide input and requirements to other services as required.

(b) Manage the assignment of parachuting-related formal school quotas via the Student Registrar Module of the Marine Corps Training Information Management System (MCTIMS) per chapter 8 of the enclosure to this Order.

(c) Evaluate the applicability and effectiveness of current and proposed USMC parachuting training programs in accordance with reference (f).

(d) Establish individual training standards for personnel parachuting and incorporate as appropriate into associated training and readiness (T&R) manuals.

(e) Participate in all parachute-related IPTs to identify and resolve training issues per chapter 2 of the enclosure to this Order.

(f) Develop, train and maintain Programs of Instruction (POI) for USMC-unique parachuting equipment as required.

(g) Provide commanders with subject matter expertise (SME)/technical assistance concerning parachuting, parachute rigging procedures, and administrative requirements during Airborne Mobile Training Team (AMTT) deployments for training (DFTs).

(h) Consult and collaborate closely with IWS/R parachute program officer in the development of manpower and training plans for parachuting equipment in RDT&E.

(i) Participate in the USMC Parachute Capabilities Conference per chapter 3 of the enclosure to this Order.

(6) <u>Commanding General, Marine Corps Systems Command (IWS/R) shall</u>:

(a) Coordinate and manage all parachute equipment research, development and acquisition as identified by DC, CD&I and validated by DC, PP&O (POG).

(b) Provide Marine Corps-wide coordination and standardization of all approved and fielded parachute systems and equipment.

(c) Serve as the Marine Corps sponsor for parachute equipment, responsible for developing and refining applicable technical and procedural techniques specific to parachute equipment, as well as developing next generation parachute equipment and monitoring/enforcing applicable safety procedures for fielded parachuting equipment.

(d) Provide assistance to DC, PP&O (POG) and CG TECOM (C461TP) with regard to parachuting safety, procedures, and techniques as requested.

(e) Participate in the USMC Parachute Capabilities Conference per chapter 3 of the enclosure to this Order.

(f) Provide MARCORSYSCOM representation for the Marine Corps in the JTAG per reference (b).

(g) Participate in all parachute-related IPTs to identify and resolve technical, systemic and/or programmatic issues per chapter 2 of the enclosure to this Order.

(7) <u>Request that Commander, Naval Safety Center (Code 44), per reference (g)</u>:

(a) Advise DC PP&O (POG), DC I&L (LPC), DC CD&I, and CG, TECOM on safety matters pertaining to personnel parachuting and air delivery procedures and techniques.

(b) Investigate and evaluate all malfunctions, incidents and parachute-related mishaps involving Marine Corps personnel and/or equipment in accordance with reference (h). Ensure compliance with reference (i), and report all violations to DC, PP&O (POG). Maintain all records per the applicable SSIC in accordance with reference (j).

(c) Maintain a data repository for all monthly airdrop reports and parachute-related malfunction/incident reports. Analyze data for trends, and distribute statistics via Naval Message to all commands with parachuting capabilities on a semi-annual basis, at a minimum.

(d) Participate in the USMC Parachute Capabilities Conference per chapter 3 of the enclosure to this Order.

(e) Attend all Army, Navy, Air Force, and Marine Corps parachute-related Malfunction Review Boards. Attend DOD and civilian conferences related to personnel parachute and cargo airdrop equipment (as appropriate) as the Marine Corps parachute safety subject matter expert.

(f) Conduct parachute safety inspections on all Marine Corps units with a parachute capability at least once every 2 years. Conduct safety surveys or assist visits as requested by units, or as directed by DC, PP&O (POG) or DC, I&L (LPC).

(g) Participate in all parachute-related IPTs to identify and resolve safety issues per chapter 2 of the enclosure to this Order.

(h) Publish and maintain a listing of all current publications pertinent to parachute and air delivery operations, training and maintenance.

(i) Evaluate OT and DT of procedures for personnel parachuting and air delivery for USMC aircraft in RDT&E.

(j) Upon completion of OT and DT of procedures for personnel parachuting and air delivery for USMC aircraft in RDT&E, issue a Safety Confirmation to DC, PP&O (POG) certifying the accepted procedures as safe and reliable for DOD use.

(8) <u>Marine Corps Commanders/Officers-in-Charge of formal training units/activities shall</u>:

(a) Administer, manage and oversee formal courses of instruction in accordance with reference (d).

(b) Ensure all parachute training and operations are conducted in accordance with reference (k). In situations where proponent operational risk management (ORM) procedures have not adequately mitigated identified risks, report discrepancies and possible safety issues to DC, PP&O (POG).

(c) Ensure parachute operations are conducted and supervised by a current Jumpmaster trained on the type of equipment used for each training evolution.

(d) Ensure all instructor and student certification, recertification and refresher training is conducted and documented per the enclosure to this Order.

(9) <u>Unit Commanders shall</u>:

(a) Ensure and enforce compliance with this Order and all other applicable directives within their purview.

(b) Ensure currency and qualification of all parachutists and Jumpmasters per the enclosure to this Order.

(c) Ensure certification, recertification and refresher training is conducted and documented as required per the enclosure to this Order.

(d) Ensure proper maintenance, inspection, security and storage of all parachute equipment per this Order, applicable references and equipment technical manuals referenced in the enclosure to this Order.

(e) Develop and maintain a unit Standard Operating Procedure (SOP) for parachute operations, addressing specific areas not addressed in current directives or doctrinal publications.

5. <u>Administration and Logistics</u>

a. Exceptions to Policy. Requests to waive or permanently change any portion of this Order will be submitted via the first O-5 in the chain of command to DC, PP&O (POG) per chapter 5 of the enclosure to this Order.

b. Definitions. For the purposes of this Order, the following phrases or terms apply:

(1) Marine Corps Personnel. This phrase refers to all active, reserve and civilian employed USMC personnel, USMC contractors and any DOD uniformed military personnel assigned to Marine Corps units.

(2) Marine Corps Parachute Operations and Training. This phrase refers to parachute and/or aerial delivery of cargo operations and training conducted under cognizance of a Marine Corps Commander or Officer-in-Charge of a Marine Corps unit or activity.

(3) Jump. This term refers to the physical action of personnel exiting an aircraft in flight as a function of parachute operations or training.

(4) USMC-Approved Formal Course(s) of Instruction. This phrase refers to courses of instruction listed in the Marine Corps Training Information Management System (MCTIMS) Course Catalog.

6. Command and Signal

a. Command. This Order is applicable to the Marine Corps Total Force.

b. Signal. This Order is effective on the date signed.

J. F. DUNFORD, JR.
Deputy Commandant for
Plans, Policies and Operations

DISTRIBUTION: PCN 10203180000

LOCATOR SHEET

Subj: MARINE CORPS PARACHUTING POLICY AND PROGRAM ADMINISTRATION PROCEDURAL MANUAL

Location: _____

(Indicate the location(s) of the copy(ies) of this Order.)

RECORD OF CHANGES

Log completed change action as indicated.

Change Number	Date of Change	Date Entered	Signature of Person Incorporating Change

Enclosure (1)

TABLE OF CONTENTS

TABLE OF CONTENTS

Chapter 1

Proponency

1. <u>General</u>. This chapter provides detailed information on the authority, definition and scope of proponency of Marine Corps parachuting programs.

2. <u>Authority</u>. Reference (a) designates the U.S. Army as the proponent for military parachute operations common to both the Army and the Marine Corps. Reference (l) establishes USASOC as the proponent for military free-fall (MFF) training, operations, equipment, and doctrine. This Order establishes DC, PP&O (POG) as the proponent for all USMC personnel parachuting, and DC, I&L (LPC) as the proponent for USMC aerial delivery of cargo.

3. <u>Definition</u>. As proponents for their respective capability, DC, PP&O (POG) and DC, I&L (LPC) are responsible for coordination of all aspects of the development, sustainment, and maintenance of that capability and are vested with the authority to organize and direct appropriate actions to accomplish such objectives.

4. <u>Scope</u>. Tasks unique to individual proponents are identified in Paragraph 4b of this chapter. Common tasks associated with USMC parachuting proponency include, but are not limited to the following:

   a. <u>Advocacy</u>. Within their purview, proponents shall:

      (1) Serve in the role of lead advocates in the development of parachuting/air delivery capabilities per reference (m).

      (2) Serve in the role of parachuting/air delivery advocates in the development of aviation capabilities per reference (m).

      (3) Conduct inter-service coordination and liaison for Marine Corps parachute/air delivery operations and training.

      (4) Establish, direct, enforce and monitor Marine Corps integrated process teams (IPTs) to identify and resolve issues related to parachute/air delivery operations, training and equipment.

      (5) Co-sponsor the USMC Parachute Capabilities Conference per chapter 3 of this Order.

      (6) Serve in the role of Marine Corps parachuting or air delivery proponent in all matters associated with DOD executive agents.

   b. <u>Policy</u>. Within their purview, proponents shall:

      (1) Establish, enforce and monitor policy to ensure Marine Corps-wide applicability and compliance.

      (2) Serve as the sole authority to waive Marine Corps parachuting policy.

      (3) Initiate Marine Corps-wide corrective/preventative action pertaining to parachuting/air delivery as required.

Enclosure (1)

c. <u>Training</u>. Within their purview, proponents shall:

(1) Monitor and enforce proper usage of seats to formal parachuting/air delivery courses of instruction per chapter 8 of this Order.

(2) When requested by CG, Training and Education Command (TECOM), participate in the Structure/Manning Decision Review (SMDR) conducted annually by the U.S. Army Training and Doctrine Command (TRADOC).

Chapter 2

Capability Development

1. General. This chapter outlines requirements pertaining to the
development of parachuting, air delivery and aviation capabilities.

2. Parachuting and Air Delivery Capability Development. Parachuting and air
delivery capabilities will be developed to meet valid and approved
operational requirements in accordance with reference (m).

    a. Integrated Process Action Teams (IPTs). As existing parachuting or
air delivery capabilities are refined or new capabilities are developed,
proponents will establish an IPT to formally address issues arising from the
Expeditionary Force Development System Process. Many of these issues are
addressed formally through the MARCORSYSCOM Manpower & Training Plan (M&TP)
Process. During this process, the IPT assesses all doctrinal,
organizational, training, materiel, leadership and education, personnel and
facilities (DOTMLPF) implications under the guidance of the program manager
(PM). The PM uses this assessment, and any required analysis, to develcp a
plan for developing and sustaining the capability.

    b. IPT Membership. Proponents are encouraged to include SMEs from
across DOD in the development of parachute and air delivery capabilities;
however, IPT's formed for this purpose will consist of, at a minimum, SME
representation from:

        (1) Proponents.

        (2) DC, CD&I (FMID/LID).

        (3) DC, Aviation (APP).

        (4) CG, Training Command (C461TP/AMTT).

        (5) CG, MARCORSYSCOM (IWS/R).

        (6) Commander, NAVSAFCEN (C 44).

    c. Proponent's Role. The proponent's role in the IPT is to ensure that
all DOTMLPF issues are addressed through facilitation and coordination of
required actions, to publish all IPT findings, with all stakeholders copied,
and when appropriate, to ensure and enable the participation of relevant
operating forces.

3. Aviation Capability Development. Parachuting and air delivery operations
from newly developed aviation assets require official authorization from the
appropriate DOD parachuting EA. Direct involvement of the Marine Corps
parachuting and air delivery proponents is critical to effective inter-
service coordination in gaining this authorization. At a minimum, this
authorization requires the following:

    a. Official parachute and air delivery testing by a recognized DOD test
and evaluation organization. This will involve test and evaluation of
current parachuting and air delivery procedures, as well as the development
of any changes or new procedures.

    b. The appropriate Service safety organization's Safety Confirmation to
conduct parachute and air delivery operations from the newly developed
aircraft using any new or changed parachuting or air delivery procedures.
This Safety Confirmation applies to the parachuting and/or air delivery
procedures and is separate from the test and evaluation organization's
assessment of the aircraft for safety and suitability.

    c. An official service-level request both to authorize parachuting and
air delivery operations from the newly developed aircraft, and to implement
validated changes/additions to procedures in the appropriate publications and
directives.

Chapter 3

USMC Parachute Capabilities Conference

1. <u>General</u>. This chapter provides detailed information on the purpose, sponsorship, participants, and actions of the USMC Parachute Capabilities Conference.

2. <u>Purpose</u>. The USMC Parachute Capabilities Conference convenes annually and serves as a forum for the presentation of relevant parachuting and air delivery capability issues requiring proponent or HQMC action and the development of detailed Plans of Action and Milestones (POA&Ms) to resolve those issues.

3. <u>Sponsorship</u>. The USMC Parachute Capabilities Conference is co-sponsored by DC, PP&O (POG) and DC, I&L (LPC). Sponsorship includes, but is not limited to, the following:

   a. Agenda Development.

   b. Administrative and Logistical Coordination.

   c. Conference Facilitation.

   d. Development of Conference Messages.

4. <u>Participants</u>. Units listed in chapter 4, Paragraph 2a of this Order are standing members of the USMC Parachute Capabilities Conference. Each of these units will send a designated parachuting SME to represent his command. Attending SMEs must be empowered to speak on behalf of their commanders regarding all conference agenda items. In addition to the co-sponsors, representation from each of the following is also required:

   a. DC, CD&I (FMID/LID).

   b. DC, Aviation (APP).

   c. CG, Training Command (C461TP/AMTT).

   d. CG, MARCORSYSCOM (IWS/R).

   e. Commander, NAVSAFCEN (C 44).

   f. Commanding Officer, Marine Corps Detachment, Fort Benning.

   g. Commanding Officer, Marine Corps Detachment, U.S. Army Special Operations Command (USASOC) JFK Special Warfare Center and School (JFKSWCS).

   h. Commanding Officer, Marine Corps Detachment, Fort Lee.

5. <u>Actions</u>. At a minimum, the following actions will take place:

   a. Sponsors will facilitate the conference by ensuring that the agenda is established, published and followed.

   b. Attendees will receive a MARCORSYSCOM update on all current programs of record, as well as any RDT&E efforts to develop approved capabilities.

c. Working groups will be established to address specific issues and to develop recommended courses of action as required.

d. Sponsors will develop a conference message containing the final disposition of all agenda items.

Chapter 4

Organization

1. General. This chapter provides detailed information on the policy,
definitions, authorities, responsibilities, and procedures associated with
the organization of Marine Corps parachuting programs.

2. Unit Types. The following unit types have a valid requirement to develop
and maintain a viable parachuting capability to support prescribed missions
and approved concepts of operations using equipment organic to the
organization:

    a. Reconnaissance Battalions.

    b. Force Reconnaissance Companies.

    c. Air Delivery Platoons.

    d. Radio Reconnaissance Platoons.

    e. Reserve Component Air Naval Gunfire Liaison Companies (ANGLICO).

    f. Training and Education Command.

    g. Marine Corps Systems Command.

    h. Marine Forces Special Operations Command (MARSOC).

3. Parachutist Billets. Reference (n) identifies and codifies all skill
requirements for Marines. Reference (o) identifies and codifies skill and
qualification requirements for Navy personnel. Authorized Marine Corps
parachutist billets are indicated on unit Tables of Organization (T/Os) by
one of the following military occupational specialties (MOS) or Navy enlisted
classification (NEC) codes:

    a. 0323, Reconnaissance Man, Parachute Qualified.

    b. 0326, Reconnaissance Man, Parachute and Combatant Diver Qualified.

    c. 0451, Parachute Rigger.

    d. 8023, Parachutist.

    e. 8026, Parachutist/Combatant Diver Marine.

    f. 8403, Fleet Marine Force Reconnaissance Independent Duty Corpsman.

    g. 8427, Fleet Marine Force Reconnaissance Corpsman.

4. Table of Organization and Equipment Change Requests (TOECR). TOECRs are
submitted in accordance with reference (p). All TOECRs involving parachutist
billets or parachute equipment will be forwarded to DC, PP&O (POG) for
concurrence prior to approval.

Chapter 5

Administration

1. <u>General</u>. This chapter provides detailed information on the policy, definitions, authorities, responsibilities, and procedures associated with administration of Marine Corps parachute programs.

2. <u>Insignia</u>

   a. <u>Basic Parachutist Insignia</u>. Marine Corps personnel qualified as basic parachutists are authorized to wear the Basic Parachutist Insignia in accordance with reference (q).

   b. <u>Navy and Marine Corps Parachutist Insignia</u>. In accordance with reference (q), Marine Corps personnel qualified as basic parachutists may wear the Navy and Marine Corps Parachutist Insignia in place of the Basic Parachutist Insignia after fulfilling any one of the requirements below.

      (1) Marine Corps personnel completing five (5) additional jumps while assigned to an authorized T/O parachuting billet for a period of no less than ninety (90) days. The five (5) additional jumps must include at least one (1) combat equipment day jump, two (2) combat equipment night jumps, and employ at least two (2) different types of military aircraft.

      (2) Marine Corps personnel who are commissioned graduates of the U.S. Naval Academy (USNA), meeting the following criteria:

         (a) As a member of the USNA Airborne Training Unit, completes a USMC-approved jumpmaster and/or parachute rigger course and participates extensively for at least a year in those capacities.

         (b) Completes a minimum of 30 static line parachute jumps, to include the same variety of jumps and aircraft described above.

         (c) Has a written request to wear the Navy and Marine Corps Parachutist Insignia, endorsed by the USNA Marine Corps Representative, and approved by the CG, MCCDC (C443).

      (3) Marine Corps personnel with prior service in other branches of the U.S. Armed Forces meeting the following criteria during the period of prior service:

         (a) While assigned to an authorized (assigned by orders and receiving Parachutist HDIP) parachuting billet, fulfilled the Marine Corps criteria regarding the number, type, and frequency of parachute jumps above.

         (b) Has submitted a written request to wear the Navy and Marine Corps Parachutist Insignia, forwarded through the chain of command, and approved by the CG, MCCDC (C443). Substantiating documentation will include:

            <u>1</u>. Certified true copies of jump manifests;

            <u>2</u>. Certified true copy of DD Form 214, and/or other documents attesting to the fulfillment of Marine Corps criteria.

     <u>3</u>. Certified true copy of orders to duty involving parachuting or authorization to receive incentive pay.

     (4) Marine Corps personnel completing one combat parachute jump of any kind from any aircraft, regardless of T/O billet.

    c. <u>Exceptions</u>. Requests for authority to wear the Basic Parachutist or Navy and Marine Corps Parachutist Insignia in cases not covered above will be forwarded via the chain of command to the CG, MCCDC (C443), Quantico, VA 22134-5001, for approval.

    d. <u>Manner of Display</u>. Marine Corps personnel authorized to wear parachutist insignia will do so in compliance with reference (r) and any subsequent applicable Marine Corps bulletins in the 1020 series.

3. <u>Assignment and Voiding of Military Occupational Specialties</u>

    a. Marine Corps personnel are assigned the corresponding parachutist AMOS upon successful completion of the appropriate formal course of instruction. Local administration offices will make the appropriate unit diary entries in MCTFS only after substantiating documentation is provided.

    b. Marine Corps personnel possessing PMOSs 0451 and 0405 are qualified parachutists and will not be assigned AMOS 8023.

    c. Requirements, procedures and authority for voiding a parachutist MOS are found in reference (q) and paragraph 10 of this chapter. In addition to the requirements in the references, Marine Corps personnel may have the parachutist designation revoked in the event of severe safety violations or gross negligence.

4. <u>Swim Qualification</u>. Due to water hazards on and near parachute drop zones, Marine Corps personnel filling valid parachuting billets and/or participating in parachute training on a permissive basis must be qualified as CWS-2 at a minimum. Commanders will make every effort to qualify all parachutists as CWS-1. All Marine Corps personnel participating in deliberate water parachute operations will be qualified as CWS-1, per reference (s).

5. <u>Marine Corps Total Force System (MCTFS) Entries</u>

    a. Formal Schools. Upon successful completion and MCTIMS validation of the formal courses of instruction listed below, the corresponding Service School Code (SSC) will be entered on the education page in MCTFS.

     (1) Airborne (A030CG1)......................................0CG

     (2) MFF Parachutist (A0571F1)............................71F

     (3) Jumpmaster (A0371M1)..................................71M

     (4) MFF Jumpmaster (A0571P1).............................71P

     (5) Parachute Rigger Course (A1471H1)...................71H

     (6) Ram-Air Parachute Systems (A14LBE1).................LBE

(7) MC-5 RAPS Static Line Transition Course (M02KAZM)....KAZ

(8) MC-5 RAPS Static Line Jumpmaster Course (M0271RM)....71R

(9) MC-5 RAPS Rigger Course (M02LBVM)....................LBV

(10) TORDS Equipment Course (CID M02KAYM)...............KAY

(11) TORDS Personnel Course (CID M02KA3M)...............KA3

   b. Other Training. Formal courses of instruction still in development
or those conducted under the umbrella of new equipment training (NET) have
neither a SSC nor a MCTIMS course identification code (CID). Some examples
of such training are listed in chapter 7 of this Order. Because this
training prepares and certifies Marine Corps personnel to perform specific
skills or to use specific equipment, successful completion of this training
requires official documentation. In such instances, commanders will ensure
this training is documented under the Local Schools section of the MCTFS
education page.

6. Appointments, Orders and Authorizations. Commanders will assign Marine
Corps personnel to parachute duties commensurate with their billet, training
and qualifications. When required, unit special orders and/or certification
letters may serve as source documents for reporting eligibility for
Parachutist Hazardous Duty Incentive Pay and applicable unit diary entries.

   a. Parachute Duty. Qualified Marine Corps personnel filling valid
parachutist billets will be ordered to parachute duty in writing. Orders may
be issued individually or collectively, however all Marine Corps personnel
assigned to parachute duty will be assigned by-name to specific parachutist
billets, and billets will be designated by specific billet identification
code (BIC) as assigned by the Total Force Structure Management System
(TFSMS). An example of parachute duty orders can be found in figure 5-1 of
this Order, however this serves as only a guide. Commanders may issue orders
to duty in the most appropriate official format available.

   b. Command Jumpmaster

      (1) Commanders will appoint appropriately qualified Marine Corps
personnel, Corporal and above, as command jumpmasters upon qualification in
accordance with chapter 7 of reference (s) or chapter 13 of reference (t), as
well as any additional (more stringent) unit-level jumpmaster requirements.
Qualified Marine Corps personnel will be appointed in writing as command
jumpmasters. Appropriately qualified and appointed jumpmasters are
authorized to function in the capacity of primary jumpmaster, assistant
jumpmaster, safety, departure airfield control officer, or drop zone safety
officer/team leader. An example of an appointment as a command jumpmaster
can be found in figure 5-2 of this Order.

      (2) Appointment as a command jumpmaster applies only to parachute
operations under the cognizance of the appointing commander. Command
jumpmasters from one unit are not authorized to perform any jumpmaster duties
during parachute operations of another unit unless explicitly authorized to
do so in writing by the commander conducting the operation.

   c. Command Parachute Safety Officer (PSO). Commanders will appoint, in
writing, an appropriately trained, jumpmaster-qualified, experienced

parachutist as the command PSO. Responsibilities and requirements for the command PSO are detailed in chapter 7 of this Order.

    d. <u>Permissive Parachute Duty</u>

       (1) Commanders of non-parachuting units/activities are authorized to permit previously qualified parachutists and jumpmasters to participate in appropriate proficiency and refresher training under permissive orders with authorized units/activities. Permissive parachute duty orders will include documentation of appropriate qualification and medical clearance. An example of permissive parachute duty orders can be found in figure 5-4 of this Order.

       (2) Commanders of parachuting units are authorized to permit appropriately qualified personnel from other units/services to participate in parachute training under permissive parachuting orders. Commanders under whose cognizance parachute operations are conducted are responsible for ensuring all participating parachutists and jumpmasters are qualified, current and medically cleared to participate.

    e. <u>Tandem Passenger Authorization</u>. Marine Corps personnel qualified as Personnel Tandem Masters are authorized to conduct personnel tandem parachute operations and training with non-parachutist passengers. Regardless of command, tandem passengers must be authorized in writing by their commanding officer to participate in tandem parachute operations. Additional requirements for tandem passengers can be found in chapter 10, Paragraph 14 of this Order. An example of a tandem passenger authorization can be found in figure 5-5 of this Order.

7. <u>Unit/Activity Records</u>. Marine Corps units and activities described in chapter 4, paragraph 2a of this Order will maintain the following individual and unit documentation in accordance with reference (j).

    a. <u>Individual Records</u>. For Marine Corps personnel within their purview, commanders will maintain all documentation pertaining to qualification, certification, recertification, assignment and/or termination as parachutist, jumpmaster, rigger and/or command PSO in accordance with reference (j), SSIC 1320.1. Additionally, commanders will maintain copies of applicable permissive parachuting orders (with enclosures) for all personnel participating in the unit's parachute operations and training on a permissive basis in accordance with reference (j), SSIC 1320.1.

    b. <u>Unit Documentation</u>

       (1) Prior to each unit parachute operation, commanders will issue operations orders or letters of instruction, assigning in writing specific safety, support, and supervisory personnel for all aspects of that operation. Additionally, commanders will conduct and document an in-depth risk assessment in accordance with reference (k). Commanders will maintain these records in accordance with reference (j), SSIC 3500.1.

       (2) Following each parachute operation, commanders will certify all jump manifests for that operation, using figure 5-6 (OPNAV Form 3504/1) of this Order for this purpose. Figure 5-6 is available for download on Naval Forms Online at: https://navalforms.daps.dla.mil/web/public/home. Manifests will serve as the unit's sole source document for recording conduct of and participation in parachute training and is sufficient documentation of

performance of parachute duty for pay purposes. Commanders will maintain copies of manifests in accordance with reference (j), SSIC 1543.1.

(3) Commanders will maintain copies of all reports detailed in chapter 13 of this Order, as well as any additional formal correspondence pertaining to the conduct or administration of unit parachute operations or training in accordance with reference (j).

8. Individual Parachutist Logbook. Each qualified Marine Corps parachutist is required to maintain an individual parachutist log throughout his career. Logbooks will be collected by jumpmasters prior to parachute operations to verify currency and determine refresher training requirements, and are returned to parachutists upon completion. It is the responsibility of the parachutist to ensure it is updated after each parachute operation, and that it remains both accurate and current. Individual parachutist logs may be locally produced.

9. Medical

   a. Standards. Medical standards for parachute duty for Marine Corps personnel are prescribed in chapter 15-105 of reference (u). Marines undergoing U.S. Army parachutist training must also be screened using chapter 5 of reference (v).

   b. Waivers. Requests to waive medical standards for parachute duty listed in reference (u) or reference (v) will be submitted to DC, PP&O (POG) for approval via the Chief, Navy Bureau of Medicine and Surgery, Undersea Medicine & Radiation Health (M342), 2300 E. St NW, Washington, DC 20372-5300. The request will include the commander's endorsement of the medical officer's recommendation. Enclosed will be the original signed physical examination on SF-88 and personal history on SF-93. Commanders of Marines pending attendance of Basic Airborne School will send an info copy to the Commanding Officer, Marine Corps Detachment, Bldg. 4 ROOM 546, Ft Benning, GA 31905. Commanders of Marines pending attendance of the USASOC MFF School will send an info copy to the Marines Corps Representative, AOJK-L-USMC, USAJFKSWCS, Fort Bragg, NC 28310-5000.

10. Unauthorized Drug Usage and Mental Instability

   a. Any USMC parachutist, rigger or jumpmaster (qualified or in training) charged by competent civilian or military authority with unauthorized drug usage shall be relieved of all associated duties and responsibilities and prohibited access to unit paralofts, parachutes, air delivery and life support equipment. In such cases, commanders will formally notify DC, PP&O (POG), DC I&L (LPC-3) and DC, M&RA (MMEA-6). When warranted, substantiated cases may result in the voiding of the associated parachutist or rigger MOS at the discretion of the appropriate occupational field sponsor/proponent and MMEA-6.

   b. Any USMC parachutist, rigger or jumpmaster (qualified or in training) found by competent medical authority to lack the mental stability required to function in that capacity shall also be relieved of all associated duties and responsibilities and prohibited access to unit paralofts, parachutes, air delivery and life support equipment. In such cases, commanders will formally notify DC, PP&O (POG), DC I&L (LPC-3) and DC, M&RA (MMEA-6). When warranted, such cases may result in the voiding of the associated parachutist or rigger

MOS at the discretion of the appropriate occupational field sponsor/proponent and MMEA-6.

c. In any case where a rigger is relieved for cause, all parachutes, air delivery and life support equipment packed or rigged by that rigger will be identified, removed from service and secured. Such equipment will undergo a thorough technical rigger inspection prior to being placed back into service.

11. Exceptions to Policy

a. Requests to waive any portion of this order will be submitted via the first O-5 in the chain of command to DC, PP&O (POG) no later than forty-five (45) days prior to the related event. Electronic submissions of scanned requests and endorsements are recommended to increase effectiveness and minimize response time.

b. Applicable points of contact can be found on the world-wide web at http://hqinet001.hqmc.usmc.mil/pp&o/POG/Section%20Pages/recon%20page.htm. Replies to electronic requests will be returned in the same manner. Requests may be submitted via official mail, fax or electronically to the addresses below:

    (1) Commandant of the Marine Corps
        Headquarters United States Marine Corps
        Plans, Policies and Operations (POG)
        3000 Marine Corps Pentagon
        Washington, DC 20350-3000

    (2) Fax (703) 692-4430, DSN 222-4430

3500
Date

From: Commanding Officer
To: Sgt I.M. Marine, ###-##-1234/0321/0326 USMC

Subj: ASSIGNMENT TO PARACHUTE/HIGH-ALTITUDE-LOW OPENING (HALO) DUTY

Ref: (a) MCO 3120.11
      (b) MCO P1000.6G
      (c) DOD 7000.14-R, "Department of Defense Financial Management
          Regulations (FMRS)," Dates Vary by Volume
      (d) Table of Organization for UIC X#####

1. Per the references, you are hereby assigned to perform parachute/HALO
duty effective ___date___ .

2. Your billet (BIC X#############) is coded in reference (d) for parachute
duty. In accordance with references (a) through (c), you are entitled to
receive Parachutist/HALO Hazardous Duty Incentive Pay (HDIP) at the highest
rate for which you are qualified, provided you gain and maintain appropriate
minimum qualification and currency certifications. Failure to do so may
result in the termination of parachute/HALO duty status and the forfeiture of
any unauthorized HDIP payments.

3. Requirements for current and future certifications and training
progressions will be met through this or any other organization belonging to
the Department of Defense at the discretion of the individual unit commander.

4. These orders are transferable to another appropriately-coded billet in
reference (d). These orders are terminated if you are reassigned to a non-
parachutist billet, if you are found to no longer be qualified in the billet,
upon transfer from this command, or if otherwise revoked based on valid
justification.

5. It is certified that you are filling a billet that does not exceed the
number of billets authorized in reference (d) to receive Parachutist HDIP.

                           I. M. COMMANDER   .

_____

FIRST ENDORSEMENT

1. Received these orders at ___command___ on ___date___ and accept them on a
voluntary basis.

                       //s//_____

              Figure 5-1.--Sample Parachute Duty Orders

3500
Date

From: Commanding Officer
To: Sgt I.M. Marine, ###-##-1234/0321/0326 USMC

Subj: ASSIGNMENT AS COMMAND JUMPMASTER

Ref: (a) MCO 3120.11
      (b) MCWP 3-15.7, Static Line Parachuting Techniques and Training
      (c) MCWP 3-15.6, Special Forces Military Free-Fall Operations
      (d) TM 70244A-01, USMC Military Freefall Operations
      (e) Applicable Unit Special Orders

1. Per the applicable references, you are hereby assigned as a command jumpmaster effective ___date___. This assignment confers my authority to you when acting as my direct representative in the function of your duties. As such, you are directly responsible to me for the safe conduct of parachute operations within the scope of your duties for that operation.

2. This assignment authorizes you to perform only those jumpmaster duties for which you are appropriately qualified, and requires you to maintain appropriate minimum qualification and currency certifications as detailed in the references. Failure to do so will result in the automatic termination of this assignment.

3. This assignment terminates if you are found to no longer be qualified, upon transfer from this command, or if otherwise revoked based on valid justification.

4. This assignment is not to be considered as orders from competent authority for entitlement to Parachutist HDIP.

                              I. M. COMMANDER

_____

FIRST ENDORSEMENT

1. Received this assignment at ___command___ on ___date___.

                         //s//_____

                Figure 5-2.--Sample Command Jumpmaster Assignment

3500
Date

From: Commanding Officer
To: Sgt I.M. Marine, ###-##-1234/0321/0326 USMC

Subj: ASSIGNMENT AS COMMAND PARACHUTE SAFETY OFFICER

Ref: (a) MCO 3120.11
      (b) MCWP 3-15.7, Static Line Parachuting Techniques and Training
      (c) MCWP 3-15.6, Special Forces Military Free-Fall Operations
      (d) TM 70244A-01, USMC Military Freefall Operations
      (e) Applicable Unit Special Orders

1. Per the references, you are hereby assigned as the command parachute safety officer (PSO) effective ___date___. This assignment confers my authority to you when acting as my direct representative in the function of your duties. As such, you are directly responsible to me for the safe conduct of all aspects of the command's parachute program in accordance with the references. Specific responsibilities as command PSO are found in reference (a).

2. This assignment is based on your qualification and currency as a command jumpmaster and requires you to maintain appropriate minimum qualification and currency certifications as detailed in the applicable references. Failure to do so will result in the automatic termination of this assignment.

3. This assignment terminates if you are found to no longer be qualified, upon transfer from this command, or if otherwise revoked based on valid justification.

4. This assignment is not to be considered as orders from competent authority for entitlement to Parachutist HDIP.

                              I. M. COMMANDER

FIRST ENDORSEMENT

1. Received this assignment at ___command___ on ___date___.

                    //s//_____

              Figure 5-3.--Sample Command Parachute Safety Officer Assignment

3500
Date

From: Commanding Officer
To: Sgt I.M. Marine, ###-##-1234/0321/0326 USMC

Subj: PERMISSIVE PARACHUTE DUTY AUTHORIZATION

Ref: (a) MCO 3120.11
      (b) MCO P100.6G
      (c) DOD 7000.14-R, "Department of Defense Financial Management
          Regulations (FMRS)," Dates Vary by Volume
      (d) Table of Organization for UIC X#####

1. Per the references, you are hereby authorized to participate in parachute
training on a permissive basis, effective ___date___. This authorization
remains in effect until you are discharged, released or transferred from this
command, or you are no longer physically qualified to participate in such
activities.

2. This authorization serves as official orders, and is issued with the
understanding that your participation is voluntary, that you meet medical and
physical requirements to participate, and that your participation is at the
convenience of the command providing the support for such activities.

3. Acceptance of these permissive orders is not to be considered as orders
from competent authority for entitlement to Parachutist HDIP.

                              I. M. COMMANDER

FIRST ENDORSEMENT

1. Received these orders at ___command___ on ___date___ and accept them on a
voluntary basis.

                        //s//_____

Figure 5-4.--Sample Permissive Parachute Duty Authorization

3500
Date

From: Commanding Officer (of tandem passenger)
To: Sgt I.M. Marine, ###-##-1234/0321/0326 USMC

Subj: TANDEM PASSENGER AUTHORIZATION

Ref: (a) MCO 3120.11
      (b) TM 70244A-01, USMC Military Freefall Operations

1. Per the reference, you are hereby authorized to participate in tandem parachute training with __command conducting tandem jump__ on a permissive basis. This is a one-time authorization, effective for __date__ only.

2. This authorization serves as official orders, and is issued with the understanding that your participation is voluntary, that you meet medical and physical requirements to participate as indicated in the reference, and that your participation is at the convenience of both your command and the command providing the support for such activities.

3. Acceptance of these permissive orders is not to be considered as orders from competent authority for entitlement to Parachutist HDIP.

                              I. M. COMMANDER

_____
FIRST ENDORSEMENT

1. Received these orders at __command__ on __date__ and accept them on a voluntary basis.

                          //s//_____
_____
FOR TANDEM MASTER USE ONLY

Passenger Height/Weight: _____/_____   Passenger Uniform Size: _____

                                        Initials
                              Tandem Master   Passenger

Equipment Issued: _____   _____

Received Passenger Safety Brief: _____   _____

Received Equipment Brief: _____   _____

Equipment returned: _____   _____

Figure 5-5.--Sample Tandem Passenger Authorization

JUMP MANIFEST

PRIVACY ACT STATEMENT

Purpose:	Document premeditated personnel parachute jumps.
Authority:	5 USC 301, Department Regulations; OPNAVIST 3504 1, Premeditated Personnel Parachuting Log and Navy Airdrop Malfunction Report; E.O. 9397.
Routine Uses:	Document training and operational parachute jumps for statistical purposes; used to document requalification jumps and determine eligibility to receive hazardous duty pay.
Disclosure:	Voluntary. however. failure to furnish all information could delay or prevent determination of eligibility to receive hazardous duty pay.

JUMP CODES

01 = STATIC LINE SLICK
02 = STATIC LINE EQUIP
03 = HAHO S/L & F/F SLICK
04 = HAHO EQUIPMENT S/L
05 = HALO SLICK (F/F)
06 = HALO EQUIP (F/F)
07 = HALO EQUIP 02 (F/F)
08 = HAHO EQUIP (F/F)

09 = HAHO 02 F/F
10 = HAHO 02 EQUIP F/F
11 = TANDEM W/PASSENGER
12 = TANDEM W/EQUIPMENT
13 = WATER STATIC LINE
14 = WATER FREEFALL
15 = _____ * (OTHER/CANCELLATIONS)

PARACHUTE CODES

A = T-10B
B = MC1 - 1B
C = MC1 - 1C
D = A/P28S - 17
E = A/P28S - 18
F = MC - 3

G = MT - 1X8/8L
H = MT - 1XX
I = MT - 1XOCT
J = _____ * (OTHERS)

GENERAL INFORMATION

UNIT/TEAM _____ DATE _____
JUMPMASTER _____ ASST JM _____
AIRCRAFT _____ DROP ZONE _____
OIC/JUMPMASTER SIGNATURE _____

* LIST WEATHER, OPERATIONAL OR AIRCRAFT IF CODE 15 IS CANCELLATION
* FOR ANY JUMP INVOLVING AN INCIDENT EXPLAIN IN FULL ON REVERSE
* FOR TYPE JUMP PLACE CODE PRIOR TO PARACHUTE CODE (i E , 02B)

LAST NAME	SSN	DEPT	JUMP 1 TYPE	JUMP 1 ALT	JUMP 2 TYPE	JUMP 2 ALT	JUMP 3 TYPE	JUMP 3 ALT	JUMP 4 TYPE	JUMP 4 ALT	JUMP 5 TYPE	JUMP 5 ALT
1.												
2.												
3.												
4.												
5.												
6.												
7.												
8.												
9.												
10.												
11.												
12.												
13.												
14.												
15.												
16.												
17.												
18.												
19.												
20.												

OPNAV 3504/1 (Rev. 6-90)   Adobe Designer V7.0

Figure 5-6.--Jump Manifest

Chapter 6

Parachutist Hazardous Duty Incentive Pay (HDIP)

1. General

    a. This chapter provides detailed information on the policy, definitions, authorities, responsibilities, and procedures associated with Parachutist HDIP for USMC personnel.

    b. Requirements for parachute duty pay for Marine Corps personnel are set forth in volume 7A, chapter 24 of reference (w). The following information is not all-encompassing and is provided to clarify the most common issues regarding Parachutist HDIP as they are outlined in reference (w).

2. Eligibility. Marine Corps personnel who meet the criteria below are eligible to receive either Parachutist HDIP:

    a. Any Marine Corps personnel assigned to basic parachutist, MFF parachutist or parachute rigger formal qualification training;

    b. Appropriately qualified Marine Corps personnel assigned to USMC T/O billets that are coded for parachutists or parachute riggers who:

        (1) Are under competent orders to perform parachute duty.

        (2) Meet performance requirements as indicated in volume 7A, chapter 24 of reference (w).

3. Pay Rates. Qualified MFF parachutists who fill an authorized parachutist billet and meet the performance requirements are authorized to receive Parachutist HDIP at the HALO parachutist rate vice the basic parachutist rate of Parachutist HDIP.

4. Performance Requirements. Marine Corps personnel receiving Parachutist HDIP will be afforded every opportunity to meet performance requirements as prescribed in reference (w). While not all-inclusive, the scenarios below are provided to guide commanders in applying established performance requirements for pay in such a manner as to maximize benefit to the parachutist whenever possible.

    a. Rule (1). When a parachutist performs a jump during any calendar month, that parachutist qualifies for Parachutist HDIP for any consecutive three-month period that includes the month the jump was performed. For example, when a parachutist performs a jump during March 2008, he qualifies for each of the periods below. Again, commanders determine which scenario to apply based on the maximum benefit to the parachutist:

        (1) January, February and March 2008.

        (2) February, March and April 2008; or

        (3) March, April and May 2008.

    b. Rule (2). When a parachutist performs jumps during any two consecutive calendar months, a new consecutive three-month period begins with each month that a jump is made. For example, when the parachutist described under Rule (1) makes another jump during the month of April 2008, his two jumps qualify him for pay as follows:

(1) The March 2008 jump qualifies him for Parachutist HDIP for the period of January, February and March 2008; and

(2) The April 2008 jump qualifies him for Parachutist HDIP for the period of April, May and June 2008.

c. Rule (3). When a parachutist is eligible for Parachutist HDIP, but cannot meet performance requirements because of military operations or the absence of parachute equipment or aircraft, the parachutist may conduct four jumps at any time during a twelve-month period and receive Parachutist HDIP for each month of that period. The term "military operations" is undefined to give commanders broad discretion when applying this rule. This rule includes, but is not limited to, instances of scheduled and unscheduled unit or individual deployments, periods of extended unavailability such as assignment to a promotion board or the fleet assistance program (FAP), the unavailability of required aircraft due to squadron deployments or aircraft groundings, and assignment as permanent personnel to units without parachute equipment. The intent of this rule is to benefit the qualified, proficient parachutist to the maximum extent possible when situations beyond the parachutist's control prevent participation in actual parachute operations. For example, if the parachutist described under Rule (2) is assigned to a parachutist billet, is assigned to a unit with no organic parachute equipment, and is unable to make a jump during the period of July through September 2008, the parachutist qualifies for pay as indicated above, plus:

(1) The parachutist qualifies for Parachutist HDIP for the period of July 2008 through June 2009 as long as he completes four jumps at any time during the period of October 2008 through June 2009.

(2) July 2009 begins another three-month period in which the parachutist must jump. If the parachutist is unable to jump again during that three-month period, qualification for Parachutist HDIP extends for the period of July 2009 through June 2010 as long as the parachutist completes four jumps at any time during the period of October 2009 through June 2010.

d. Rule (4). Commanding officers are authorized to waive performance requirements for Parachutist HDIP for eligible parachutists who are engaged in combat operations in a hostile fire area. For parachutists who meet this requirement, commanders may waive performance requirements for any period he deems necessary until the parachutist can resume training.

e. Rule (5). The calendar month that a parachutist's parachute duty or training begins is the first month of the first consecutive three-month period referenced in Rule (1). Additionally, Parachutist HDIP is prorated for the first month of duty or training when it begins on any day other than the first day of a month.

5. Permanent Change of Station (PCS). Parachutist HDIP does not stop in instances where parachutists execute PCS orders from one hazardous duty (parachutist) billet to another. When executing PCS orders to a non-parachutist billet, Parachutist HDIP will terminate effective the date of departure from the old duty station.

6. <u>Special Requests to Award Incentive Pay</u>. Special requests to award Parachutist HDIP to Marine Corps personnel not assigned to, or in excess of, authorized T/O billets will be forwarded via the chain of command to DC PP&O (POG) for approval. Such requests require operational necessity as a justification and each will be validated on a case-by-case basis. The most common occurrence of this requirement pertains to turnover periods between incoming and outgoing personnel filling the same parachutist billet. Authorization to award Parachutist HDIP for Marine Corps personnel not assigned to, or in excess of, authorized T/O billets rests solely with DC, PP&O (POG).

Chapter 7

Qualification Requirements

1. General. This chapter provides detailed information on the policy,
definitions, authorities, responsibilities, and procedures associated with
parachuting qualification training as it pertains to Marine Corps personnel.
With the exception of USMC personnel assigned to billets within US Special
Operations Command (USSOCOM), Marine Corps personnel are authorized to attend
only USMC-approved formal parachuting-related courses of instruction, as
reflected in MCTIMS, for qualification purposes. USMC personnel assigned to
USSOCOM may attend DOD proponent-approved formal parachuting-related
qualification courses as required. Prerequisites and other administrative
requirements for USMC-approved courses are listed in course details in
MCTIMS. Upon successful completion and MCTIMS validation of approved
courses, appropriate entries in the Marine Corps Total Force System (MCTFS)
are authorized per chapter 5 of this Order.

2. Basic Parachutist. The U.S. Army Airborne Course (CID A030CG1) is the
only basic parachutist qualification course approved for attendance by Marine
Corps personnel. This course of instruction is taught on an individual basis
and qualifies personnel to participate in low-level static line parachute
operations using U.S. Army parachute equipment. Prior to using USMC-specific
parachute equipment, basic parachutists are required to undergo documented,
unit-level transition training as outlined later in this chapter.

3. Military Free Fall Parachutist. The USMC Multi-Mission Parachute System
Military Free Fall Parachutist Course (MMPC) (CID M50KLD1) is the only MFF
parachutist qualification course approved for attendance by Marine Corps
personnel. This course of instruction is taught on an individual basis and
qualifies the basic parachutist to participate in High-Altitude, Low-Opening
(HALO) and High-Altitude, High Opening (HAHO) parachute operations. Prior to
using USMC-specific parachute equipment, graduates of the USASOC MFF Course
are required to undergo a formal transition training course as outlined later
in this chapter.

4. Jumpmaster. The U.S. Army Jumpmaster Course (A0371M1) is the principal
jumpmaster qualification course approved for attendance by Marine Corps
personnel. Additional authorized jumpmaster qualification courses are
identified in chapter 7 of reference (s). Each approved jumpmaster course is
taught on an individual basis and qualifies the basic parachutist to conduct
jumpmaster duties on U.S. Army parachute equipment and to serve in jumpmaster
billets during low-level static line parachute operations in accordance with
reference (s). Only Corporals and above are eligible for assignment to
training or duty as jumpmasters. Prior to conducting jumpmaster duties on
USMC-specific parachute equipment, jumpmasters are required to undergo a
formal transition training course as outlined later in this chapter.

5. MFF Jumpmaster. The USASOC MFF Jumpmaster Course (A0571P1) is the only
MFF jumpmaster qualification course approved for attendance by Marine Corps
personnel. This course of instruction is taught on an individual basis and
qualifies the static line jumpmaster to conduct MFF jumpmaster duties on U.S.
Army parachute equipment and to perform jumpmaster duties during HALO and
HAHO parachute operations in accordance with reference (t). Integration of
the MMPS into the USASOC MFF Jumpmaster Course is scheduled to begin in
August 2009 and will be announced via Naval Message. Once integration of the
MMPS into the course is complete, USMC graduates of the USASOC MFF Jumpmaster

Course will be fully qualified to conduct MFF jumpmaster duties during MFF operations utilizing the MMPS. Prior to integration of the MMPS into the USASOC course, USMC MFF Jumpmasters conducting MFF jumpmaster duties on USMC-specific parachute equipment are required to undergo a formal transition training course as outlined later in this chapter.

6. Equipment Tandem Master. The Tandem Offset Resupply Delivery System (TORDS) Equipment Course (CID M02KAYM) is the only Equipment Tandem Master qualification course approved for attendance by Marine Corps personnel. This course of instruction is taught on an individual basis and qualifies the MFF parachutist to perform military tandem parachute delivery of equipment using the Military Tandem Vector System (MTVS) and the Military Tandem Tethered Bundle.

7. Personnel Tandem Master. The Tandem Offset Resupply Delivery System (TORDS) Personnel Course (CID M02KA3M) is the only Personnel Tandem Master qualification course approved for attendance by Marine Corps personnel. This course of instruction is taught on an individual basis and qualifies the MFF jumpmaster to perform military tandem parachute delivery of personnel using the MTVS.

8. Military Free Fall Videographer

    a. The only method of training MFF videographers is through the use of approved civilian vendor video training courses. Marine Corps personnel are authorized to attend only civilian courses taught on United States Parachute Association (USPA) affiliated drop zones and following USPA training course guidelines.

    b. Commanding Officers desiring this capability may send tandem-qualified jumpmasters and USMC civilian employees meeting USPA Standards to an approved civilian vendor video training course at the unit's expense.

    c. Successful completion of MFF videographer training will be entered in MCTFS under Local Schools. Commander's authorization letter and certification of training will be maintained locally and in SNM's Official Military Personnel File.

    d. Video equipment will not be jumped with tactical parachute systems to include the TORDS, MMPS, MC-5 or MC-4 Ram Air Parachute Systems.

    e. Jumping video equipment with any main parachute with a spring loaded pilot chute is prohibited.

    f. MFF Jumpmasters who are TORDS equipment qualified, are qualified for a USPA "C" license and have completed an approved USPA videographer course are authorized to perform videographer duties.

    g. USMC civilian employees and contractors who hold a USPA "C" license and have completed an approved USPA videographer course are authorized to perform videographer duties.

9. Parachute Rigger. The U.S. Army Parachute Rigger Course (CID A1471H1) is the only parachute rigger qualification course approved for attendance by Marine Corps personnel. This course of instruction is taught on an individual basis and qualifies personnel to pack, maintain and repair both U.S. Army and USMC parachutes and equipment. In addition, USMC civilian

employees and approved contractors serving in billets involving parachute rigger duties must hold a minimum FAA rating of Senior Rigger.

10. Parachute Pack-In-Process Inspector (PIPI)

a. The pack-in-process inspector serves as the on-site supervisor for the packing of all parachutes. The PIPI provides flexibility and safety during sustained operations and training by performing required rigger checks during the packing of parachutes by appropriately qualified parachutists. The PIPI will be assigned in writing by the commanding officer, and this assignment will be reviewed and recertified annually.

b. Requirements for PIPI qualification and certification are as follows:

(1) Current and qualified Parachute Rigger (MOS 0451) with a minimum of one year experience. USMC civilian employees and approved contractors must hold a minimum FAA rating of Senior Rigger.

(2) Corporal or above. Lance Corporals require written approval of the first Lieutenant Colonel or O-5 in the chain of command.

(3) Prior to certification as PIPI for the packing of a specific personnel parachute, PIPI candidates will satisfactorily pack that specific parachute in all configurations a minimum of twenty (20) times.

(4) Prior to certification to serve as PIPI for the packing of cargo parachutes, PIPI candidates will satisfactorily pack a minimum of fifteen (15) parachutes for the type to be certified to inspect.

11. Command Parachute Safety Officer (PSO). The unit/activity commander will appoint, in writing, an appropriately trained, jumpmaster-qualified, experienced parachutist as the command PSO to supervise the operation of the paraloft, the maintenance of parachute equipment, and the training and certification of all parachutists, riggers, and jumpmasters. The command PSO is not intended to serve as the command's parachuting subject matter expert (SME). Rather, the responsibility of the PSO is to supervise the overall safety of all parachute operations within the unit/activity. Detachments of more than thirty (30) days duration intending to exercise an airborne capability must also have an assigned PSO. With the exception of detachments of short duration, appointments will be for no less than six (6) months.

12. Malfunction Officer. Malfunction Officer requirements for static line and MFF parachute operations are defined in references (s) and (t), respectively. Personnel from other units are authorized to serve as malfunction officers for Marine Corps parachute operations. However, commanders of units conducting parachute operations and training must appoint malfunction officers in writing upon completion of local unit training regarding reference (i).

13. Prior Service Qualifications. Marine Corps personnel with prior service, regardless of branch, are subject to the requirements in this Order. Qualifications as a parachutist, jumpmaster and/or rigger via any other means than those authorized in this Order are invalid. Prior service personnel who cannot meet the qualification requirements in this Order are considered unqualified and require formal training. Exceptions to this policy are authorized by the respective USMC parachuting proponent only.

14. <u>USMC-Specific Equipment Training</u>. Due to the high risk nature of parachuting, parachutists and jumpmasters qualified on U.S. Army parachute equipment are not qualified to perform duties using equipment unique to the Marine Corps until undergoing prescribed equipment-specific training. This training is developed during the Manpower and Training Plan (MTP) development process, and provides for new equipment training (NET) for existing parachutists, jumpmasters and riggers under the purview of CG MARCORSYSCOM. Reference (x) serves as the authoritative reference publication for parachutists, jumpmasters and riggers on USMC-specific parachuting equipment in the absence of a corresponding reference promulgated by the DOD proponent. NET normally spans a two-year period from the date of initial fielding, at which time responsibility for training the force shifts to either CG TECOM or the individual unit commanders. Current established training for USMC-specific equipment is detailed as follows.

a. <u>SF-10A Troop Back Parachute Assembly 32-Foot Diameter</u>. The SF-10A is the canopy assembly for the USMC low-level static line round parachute system. The SF-10A is currently used in conjunction with the MC1-1 personnel pack/harness assembly.

(1) <u>Parachutists</u>. Marine Corps personnel qualified as basic parachutists will undergo documented, unit-level SF-10A transition training in accordance with reference (y) prior to participating in parachute operations or training with the SF-10A. Upon completion, parachutists are completely qualified to conduct low-level static line parachute operations with the SF-10A as configured above.

(2) <u>Jumpmasters</u>. Marine Corps personnel qualified as jumpmasters must undergo no additional training to perform jumpmaster duties on the SF-10A as configured above. Jumpmasters will include the SF-10A in Pre-Jump Training as indicated in reference (y).

(3) <u>Riggers</u>. Marine Corps personnel must be qualified as parachute riggers prior to performing rigger duties on the SF-10A as configured above.

b. <u>MC-5 Ram-Air Parachute System (RAPS)</u>. The MC-5 is the legacy USMC HALO/HAHO ram-air parachute system, capable of employment as either a static line or MFF parachute.

(1) <u>Parachutists</u>

(a) <u>Static Line MC-5 RAPS Operations</u>. Marine Corps personnel qualified as basic or MFF parachutists must attend the MC-5 Ram-Air Parachute Static Line Transition Course (M02KAZM) prior to participating in static line parachute operations or training with the MC-5. This course of instruction is taught at a hosting unit by the USMC AMTT as either a stand-alone individual qualification course or in conjunction with and as a precursor to a unit HAHO training package. During the conduct of this course, parachutists are instructed and required to pack the MC-5 RAPS under the supervision of a Pack-in-Process Inspector (PIPI). Upon completion, parachutists are qualified to conduct HAHO static line parachute operations with the MC-5 RAPS.

(b) <u>MFF MC-5 RAPS Operations</u>. Marine Corps personnel qualified as MFF parachutists must attend documented, unit-level MC-5 familiarization training prior to participating in MFF parachute operations or training with the MC-5. While this training is not standardized, it should cover the differences in form and function between the MC-4 and MC-5 (and associated equipment) at a minimum. No additional formal training is required.

(2) Jumpmasters

(a) Static Line MC-5 RAPS Operations. Marine Corps personnel qualified as static line jumpmasters must attend the MC-5 Ram-Air Parachute System Jumpmaster Course (M0271RM) prior to performing jumpmaster duties on the MC-5 RAPS. This course of instruction is taught at a hosting unit by the USMC AMTT as either a stand-alone individual qualification course or in conjunction with and as a precursor to a unit HAHO training package. Upon completion, parachutists are qualified to supervise HAHO static line parachute operations with the MC-5 RAPS.

(b) MFF MC-5 RAPS Operations. Marine Corps personnel qualified as MFF jumpmasters must attend documented, unit-level MC-5 familiarization training prior to participating in MFF parachute operations or training with the MC-5. No additional formal training is required.

(3) Riggers. Marine Corps personnel qualified as parachute riggers must attend the USMC MC-5 Ram-Air Parachute System Rigger Course (M02LBVM) prior to performing rigger duties on the MC-5 RAPS. This course of instruction is taught at a hosting unit by the USMC AMTT as either a stand-alone individual qualification course or in conjunction with and as a precursor to a unit HAHO training package. Upon completion, riggers are qualified to perform rigger duties on the MC-5 RAPS.

c. Multi-Mission Parachute System (MMPS). The MMPS is the replacement HALO/HAHO Ram-Air Parachute System for the MC-5, capable of employment as a static line parachute in the double-bag static line (DBSL) configuration, and as a MFF parachute in the hand-deployed pilot chute (HDPC), self-set drogue and the static line drogue configurations. All qualification training for the MMPS is currently sourced by CG MARCORSYSCOM as a function of established New Equipment Training (NETT). Responsibility for this training becomes that of CG TECOM in FY2010 in accordance with the MMPS Manpower and Training Plan.

(1) Parachutists

(a) Static Line MMPS Operations. Marine Corps personnel qualified as basic parachutists must attend the MMPS Static Line Transition Course (CID pending) prior to participating in static line parachute operations or training with the MMPS. This course of instruction is taught at a hosting unit by the USMC AMTT as either a stand-alone individual qualification course or in conjunction with and as a precursor to a unit HAHO training package. During the conduct of this course, parachutists are instructed and required to pack the MMPS in the DBSL configuration under the supervision of a Pack-in-Process Inspector (PIPI). Upon completion, parachutists are qualified to conduct HAHO static line parachute operations with the MMPS in the DBSL configuration only.

(b) MFF MMPS Operations. Marine Corps personnel qualified as MFF parachutists at the USASOC MFF Course (CID A0571F1) must attend the MMPS Free Fall Parachutist Transition Course prior to participating in MFF parachute operations or training with the MMPS. During the conduct of this course, parachutists are instructed and required to pack the MMPS in all configurations under the supervision of a Pack-in-Process Inspector (PIPI). In lieu of the MMPS Free Fall Parachutist Transition Course, Marines may attend the MMPC for qualification as a MMPS MFF Parachutist. These courses of instruction are taught on an individual basis and qualify personnel to participate in HAHO/HALO parachute operations using the MMPS (using the MP-360 canopy only) in all configurations listed above. On request, the USMC AMTT will conduct a Special Application Parachute (SAP) Canopy Pilot Course (CID pending) for select MMPS-qualified MFF parachutists. This course of instruction is taught on an individual basis at a hosting unit and qualifies MFF parachutist to employ the MMPS using the HG-380 SAP canopy.

      (2) <u>Jumpmasters</u>. Marine Corps personnel qualified as MFF jumpmasters at the USASOC MFF Jumpmaster Course prior to integration of the MMPS into the USASOC Course must successfully complete the MMPS Jumpmaster Transition Course prior to performing jumpmaster duties on the MMPS. The MMPS Jumpmaster Transition Course is conducted at the unit level utilizing the MARCORSYCOM Course Conduct Publication for the MMPS Jumpmaster Transition Course. Upon completion, MFF jumpmasters are completely qualified to perform jumpmaster duties during HALO and HAHO parachute operations with the MMPS in all configurations, regardless of canopy.

      (3) <u>Riggers</u>. Marine Corps personnel successfully completing the U.S. Army Parachute Rigger Course (CID A1471H1) after 1 August 2008 are qualified to perform rigger duties on the MMPS in the Double Bag Static Line configuration. Rigger training on the Hand Deployed Pilot Chute, Static Line Drogue, and Self Set Drogue configurations, as well as the SAP will be conducted via the MARCORSYSCOM NETT until the Army Parachute Rigger Course incorporates these configurations into the course. Riggers who completed PMOS 0451 training prior to 1 August 2008 receive MMPS-specific formal qualification instruction via the MARCORSYSCOM NETT.

Chapter 8

Formal Training Requirements and School Seat Management

1. <u>General</u>. This chapter provides detailed information on the policy, definitions, authorities, responsibilities, and procedures associated with parachute formal training requirements and school seat management for Marine Corps personnel.

2. <u>Formal Training Requirements</u>

　　a. Marine Corps seats to DOD parachuting courses are used exclusively to train Marine Corps personnel assigned to authorized billets, or in receipt of official orders to such billets, except as indicated in paragraph 2b below. Authorized billets are defined in chapter 4 of this Order.

　　b. Training requirements for units identified in chapter 4 of this Order and CMC-approved enlistment/retention incentives are presented to and validated by CG, TECOM, Formal Schools Training Branch (C4611) via the TIP process in accordance with reference (f). DC, PP&O (POG) will validate and prioritize requirements for personnel parachuting courses as requested by CG, TECOM (C4611).

3. <u>Formal Training Allocations</u>. Seats to formal parachuting courses of instruction are allocated by CG, TECOM (C4611) to major commands and occupational field sponsors (OFS) based on operational necessity. Major commands and OFSs with allocated seats are encouraged to coordinate one-for-one exchanges of assigned seats in order to resolve scheduling conflicts caused by operational and deployment tempo, and are required to report all exchanges to CG TECOM (C4611) for inclusion into the Training Quota Memorandum (TQM) via a TQM change.

4. <u>Unprogrammed Requirements and Late Requests</u>

　　a. <u>Unprogrammed Requirements</u>. Allocated seats are intended to fill stated and validated requirements only, however urgent and/or unique operational requirements may merit exception to policy. Requests for exception to this policy will be submitted via the chain of command to DC, PP&O (POG) per chapter 5 of this Order, and each will be considered on a case-by-case basis. These requests are both unbudgeted and un-programmed, are not eligible for funding by the Worldwide TAD (WWTAD) Fund and require unit TAD funding to execute.

　　b. <u>Late Requests</u>. Requests to attend parachuting courses of instruction submitted later than ten (10) working days prior to the published report date are considered late requests. Late requests are not eligible for funding by the Worldwide TAD (WWTAD) Fund and require unit TAD funding to execute.

5. <u>Incentive Allocations</u>. The use of seats to entry-level parachuting courses as a reenlistment incentive may be authorized, based on the availability of quotas sponsored by DC, M&RA. Requests will be submitted through the chain of command, to DC, M&RA (MMEA-6) for approval and funding.

6. Vacant Formal School Seats

    a. Seats to any parachuting courses that remain unfilled fifty (50) days prior to the published report date will be recouped by DC, PP&O (POG) for reclassification and reallocation via MCTIMS.

    b. On occasion, seats to parachuting courses may become available due to late cancellations. When solicited by DC, PP&O (POG), commanders of units and personnel meeting the criteria specified in chapter 4 of this Order are encouraged to use these seats provided that unit TAD funds are used and all Marine Corps funded and programmed seats are filled.

7. Formal School Attendance in a Permissive Temporary Additional Duty Status. Marine Corps personnel are not authorized to attend formal parachute courses of instruction while in a Permissive TAD status, and must be ordered to parachute duty by competent authority.

Chapter 9

Proficiency and Refresher Training

1. General. This chapter provides detailed information on the policy, definitions, authorities, responsibilities, and procedures associated with parachute proficiency and refresher training for Marine Corps personnel.

2. Limitations on Proficiency Training. Only DOD personnel who successfully complete USMC-approved parachuting courses of instruction may participate in Marine Corps parachute operations or training, and participation is limited to the duties and type of operation and equipment for which the individual is qualified. USMC civilian employees and contractors with job/position descriptions including parachute duty must also hold a minimum USPA "C" license to participate in USMC parachute operations. Unless certified by the appropriate service proponent, foreign and civilian courses of instruction are not recognized due to the Marine Corps' limited ability to ensure DOD executive agent standards for equipment and training are met and maintained.

3. Requirements for Proficiency and Refresher Training. Parachuting skills are perishable and require periodic sustainment training to maintain proficiency. Minimum proficiency and refresher training requirements for qualified Marine Corps parachutists and jumpmasters assigned to valid parachutist billets are identified below. Proficiency requirements are intended to sustain basic individual proficiency only, and not advanced individual skills or unit capabilities. Commanders may issue more stringent proficiency and/or refresher training requirements via unit directives as required. These requirements are unrelated to Parachutist Hazardous Duty Incentive Pay (HDIP).

    a. Basic Parachutists. Both proficiency and refresher training requirements for basic parachutists are defined in appendix A of reference (s). All Marine Corps personnel returning from initial qualification training as basic parachutists are required to conduct refresher training prior to first participating in Marine Corps parachute operations and training. Additionally, the first jump after completion of initial basic parachutist qualification training will be conducted administratively, during daylight, on land, and without combat equipment.

    b. MFF Parachutists. Both proficiency and refresher training requirements for MFF parachutists are defined in reference (t).

    c. Static Line Jumpmasters. Proficiency and refresher training requirements for static line jumpmasters are defined in chapter 7 and appendix C respectively of reference (s).

    d. MFF Jumpmasters. Proficiency and refresher training requirements for MFF jumpmasters are defined in chapter 13 of reference (t).

4. Responsibilities

    a. Parachutists. When manifesting for Marine Corps parachute operations, parachutists are required to inform the primary jumpmaster if that jump will be their first jump following either initial qualification training or any 6-month lapse in proficiency training.

b. Jumpmasters. While parachutists are required to inform the primary jumpmaster as detailed in the previous Paragraph, it is the responsibility of the primary jumpmaster to ensure that all parachutists are both qualified and current to conduct the planned operations.

5. Permissive Parachute Training

a. Purpose. Commanders of units without a parachuting capability are encouraged to afford qualified Marine Corps parachutists the opportunity to maintain currency and qualification when feasible. Likewise, commanders of units with a parachuting capability are also encouraged to afford qualified Marine Corps parachutists the opportunity to participate in unit training when practical. Qualified Marine Corps parachutists and jumpmasters have no requirement to conduct proficiency training when assigned to billets with no parachutist requirements. However, when authorized by their commander to participate in parachute operations and training on a permissive basis, all proficiency and refresher training requirements apply, including any additional requirements of the host unit.

b. Requirements for Participation. Participation of Marine Corps personnel in Marine Corps parachute operations and training on a permissive basis may be conditionally authorized by the commander of the unit conducting the operations. Criteria for such participation are as follows:

(1) An appropriate qualification course, as detailed in this Order, has been successfully completed by each participant and validated by the commander of the unit conducting the parachute operations/training.

(2) Participants possess written authorization to participate in such operations/training on a permissive and not-to-interfere basis from their own operational commander in accordance with chapter 4 of this Order.

(3) Participants are medically qualified to participate in the specific type of parachute operations per reference (u).

(4) After conducting an in-depth operational risk assessment, the commander of the unit conducting the parachute operations determines that such participation presents minimal and acceptable risk to all participants.

Chapter 10

Unit Training and Operational Requirements

1. General. This chapter provides detailed information on the policy, definitions, authorities, responsibilities, and procedures associated with unit requirements pertaining to parachute training.

2. Drop Zones. All drop zones used by Marine Corps personnel will be surveyed and established as required in references (s) and (t), regardless of location. This includes all drop zones in the United States and Foreign countries.

3. C-130 Over-the-Ramp Static Line Parachute Operations. All units authorized to conduct static line parachute operations are authorized to conduct over-the-ramp operations with the C-130 aircraft as prescribed in reference (s).

4. Deliberate Water Parachute Operations. Requirements and procedures for deliberate water parachute operations are detailed in reference (s). Additional requirements for deliberate water parachute operations are as follows:

    a. All recovery boats required for the operation will be on station with engines running prior to the release of parachutists.

    b. Safety swimmers will have a thorough understanding of parachute characteristics in the water and will be proficient in the removal of parachute equipment from parachutists in that environment.

5. Debriefs. Jumpmasters will conduct a detailed after-action debrief prior to the conclusion of each parachute operation. This debrief will cover the observations, lessons-learned and recommendations for future operations of all key personnel and participants.

6. Medical Support. Medical support personnel for Marine Corps parachute operations will be assigned no other duties for the operation which they support. In the event that assigned medical support personnel are required to leave the drop zone, parachute operations will cease until medical support requirements are satisfied.

    a. U.S. Navy Personnel. Military medical support for Marine Corps parachute operations may consist of U.S. Navy personnel from NEC 8403/04/25/27/91/92/93, as well as medical officers.

    b. Other Services' Personnel. Military medical support for Marine Corps parachute operations may consist of uniformed personnel from other services with trauma training equivalent to that of an Emergency Medical Technician (EMT).

    c. Civilian Personnel. Civilian medical support for Marine Corps parachute operations must consist of personnel licensed as EMTs or higher. Civilian medical support may be used when military medical support is not available (e.g. Marine Corps Base Fire Departments/EMT units).

7. Parachute Re-Pack

   a. Units conducting sustained parachute operations or training may allow the appropriately qualified ram-air parachutist to re-pack his own main RAPS canopy under the direct supervision of a current PIPI.

   b. Parachutists will not jump parachutes packed by other parachutists. The packing of reserve parachutes or main parachutes to be jumped by other personnel will be packed by a qualified 0451 parachute riggers or appropriately qualified and current USMC civilian employees or contractors only.

8. Sleep and Medication. Parachute operations are high-risk operations. Risk level and the probability of mishaps increase when parachutists, jumpmasters and riggers do not get sufficient rest. Therefore, commanders will ensure that all parachutists and key support personnel are afforded adequate rest prior to parachute operations and training as a function of ORM. No personnel directly involved with parachute operations shall consume alcohol within 12 hours of parachute operations. All medications used by parachutists must be approved and the parachutist cleared by the unit's medical department. The use of drugs affecting the safe conduct of parachute operations is strictly prohibited.

9. Participation of Marine Corps Personnel with Other Services and Agencies. Following an in-depth risk assessment, unit commanders and officers-in-charge may authorize qualified and current Marine Corps personnel in their charge to participate in parachuting operations conducted by other U.S. military services or agencies.

10. Participation of Marine Corps Personnel with Foreign Military Services. Following an in-depth risk assessment, participation of qualified and current Marine Corps personnel in parachute operations conducted by foreign military services using foreign military equipment may be authorized in writing by the first Lieutenant Colonel or O-5 in the chain of command.

11. Participation of Non-Marine Corps Personnel in Marine Corps Parachute Operations. Following an in-depth risk assessment, Marine Corps unit commanders and officers-in-charge may authorize participation of other appropriately qualified DOD uniformed personnel, U.S. Government civilian employees, MARCORSYSCOM-approved contractors, MCCDC-approved contractors, MEF/DIV-approved life support maintenance technician contractors, and foreign military personnel in Marine Corps parachute operations. Upon meeting all criteria for participation in permissive parachute operations per chapter 9 of this Order, such personnel may be authorized in writing to participate in Marine Corps parachute operations by the first O-5 in the chain of command of the unit conducting the parachute operations.

12. Personnel Tandem Parachute Operations

   a. Commanders will ensure tandem passengers for personnel tandem parachute operations and training have current, by-name authorization per chapter 5 of this Order.

   b. Tandem parachute passengers will be in a full-duty medical status. In addition, for tandem parachute operations and training above 10,000 ft. MSL, commanders will ensure tandem passengers have a current class II flight physical and a current AF Form 702 or AF Form 1274 (HAPS card).

c. Passengers for tandem parachute training will be uniformed, DOD personnel only. Status of passengers for combat tandem parachute operations will vary by mission as required.

13. <u>Combat Operations</u>

a. Authority to waive safety policy and/or prescribed operating procedures for personnel or cargo airdrop during combat operations rests with the first General Officer in the chain of command. In situations where gaining General Officer approval may jeopardize mission success, the first Lieutenant Colonel or O-5 in the chain of command may authorize specific deviations from established policy or procedure.

b. For all instances of waiving or deviating from established policy or procedure, the appropriate USMC proponent will be officially notified via Naval Message as soon as possible.

14. <u>Participation in Community Relations Activities</u>. Participation of Marine Corps parachutists in community relations activities such as air shows and other demonstrations is governed by reference (ad). In instances where this Order and reference (ad) conflict, the requirement imposing the safest requirement takes precedence.

Chapter 11

Parachute Equipment

1. General. This chapter provides detailed information on the policy, definitions, authorities, responsibilities, and procedures associated with parachute equipment.

2. Authorized Users and Maintainers

    a. Only Marine Corps units and activities with an authorized allowance of parachute equipment on their Table of Equipment (T/E) are authorized to possess and maintain parachute equipment or to conduct parachute operations.

    b. Marine Corps units and activities with authorized parachutist billets, but lacking equipment allowances, may be supported on a not-to-interfere basis, based on operational mission requirements, by the nearest appropriate Marine Corps unit or activity possessing the appropriate equipment.

3. Authorized Equipment. Only equipment found in reference (z) and in appropriate Marine Corps stock lists is authorized for use by Marine Corps personnel in military parachuting.

4. Restrictions and Limitations on Use of Equipment

    a. Government-Owned Equipment. Government-owned parachute equipment will be used for approved military operations only and will not be used for off-duty activities.

    b. Personally-Owned Equipment. The use of personally-owned parachutes during Marine Corps parachute operations is prohibited. Personally-owned parachutes will not be used from military aircraft.

5. Parachute Packing Requirements

    a. Except where directed in this Order, only qualified and current parachute riggers with the PMOS/AMOS of 0451 or approved USMC civilian parachute riggers are authorized to pack, maintain, and store parachute equipment in accordance with technical manuals for that specific parachute equipment.

    b. At a minimum, two appropriately qualified parachute riggers (military or civilian) are required to pack and maintain parachute life support equipment- one to pack, and one to inspect. This requirement applies to all units, in garrison and deployed. Parachutes will not be embarked with deploying units unless accompanied by appropriately qualified parachute riggers. Parachute rigger or PIPI requirements for the packing of personnel or cargo parachutes will not be waived under any circumstances.

    c. The main parachute of the RAPS and TORDS parachute systems are the only personnel parachutes authorized to be packed by the parachutist the supervision of a current PIPI. The parachutist that packs a main parachute will be the only parachutist to jump that parachute. If a main parachute is packed by non-rigger personnel, the parachute will be repacked by the next jumper or a qualified ram-air parachute rigger prior to being jumped again.

6. Modification of Parachute Equipment. Modification of approved parachute equipment is strictly prohibited, except by authorized and qualified personnel assigned to MARCORSYSCOM or when granted by exception by DC, PP&O (POG). All modifications of parachute equipment will be conducted in accordance with a Modification Work Order and in compliance with a Safety of Use Message.

7. Defective Equipment. Parachute equipment found to be defective will be reported to CG, Marine Corps Logistics Command (LOGCOM) via the online Product Quality Deficiency Report (PQDR) process. Instructions for submitting a PQDR can be found at the following website: http://www.safetycenter.navy.mil/ashore/parachuting/default.htm. Maintenance Management Officers (MMO) will submit a copy of all parachute equipment PQDRs to CDRNAVSAFECEN (C 44) for review analysis and compilation. PQDRs can be submitted via official mail or electronically at the addresses below:

    a. Naval Safety Center (Tactical Operations)
       USMC Parachute Safety Analyst (C 44)
       375 A Street
       Norfolk, VA 23511

    b. Safe-code44@navy.mil

8. Instructor-Certified Ram-Air Parachute Systems (ICRAPS)

    a. Definition. ICRAPS is a category of standard parachute equipment procured for use exclusively by authorized personnel cited in subparagraph 8c below. As standard equipment, all RDT&E is complete and the system has been officially procured and fielded to specific Marine Corps units.

    b. Description and Purpose. The current USMC ICRAPS is the Military Tandem Training Vector System (MTTVS), named for its primary function as a proficiency and refresher training mechanism for qualified tandem masters. ICRAPS is also used by extremely qualified and proficient parachutists to video and perform freefall maneuvers in close proximity to other parachutists requiring refresher training.

    c. Authorized Users. Only Marine Corps personnel, other appropriately qualified DOD uniformed personnel, USMC civilian employees and approved contractors meeting the following criteria are authorized to use the ICRAPS:

       (1) MFF Jumpmasters who are TORDS equipment qualified, and who are qualified to obtain and meet the requirements for a USPA "C" license; and

       (2) USMC civilian employees and contractors who hold a USPA "C" license.

    d. Maintenance Requirements. ICRAPS will be maintained to FAA standards by appropriately credentialed ram-air riggers with a certified FAA rigger rating of senior rigger or higher. This requirement applies to military personnel and USMC civilian employees or contractors.

9. Non-standard Parachute Equipment

    a. Definition. Non-standard parachute equipment is defined as any parachute equipment for which no MARCORSYSCOM fielding plan has been approved. This equipment is still considered to be in the RDT&E process and may not yet have completed all full testing, evaluations and safety certifications. CG MARCORSYSCOM (IWS/R) is the sole owner, user, and maintainer of non-standard parachute equipment within the Marine Corps.

b. _Authorized Users_. Only appropriately qualified personnel assigned to or in direct support of MARCORSYSCOM (IWS/R) are authorized to use non-standard parachute equipment during Marine Corps parachute operations. This includes Marine Corps personnel, other DOD uniformed personnel, U.S. Government civilian employees, MARCORSYSCOM-approved contractors, MCCDC-approved contractors, and MEF/DIV-approved life support maintenance technician contractors who meet the following criteria:

(1) Possess written orders to parachuting duty and written authorization to participate in such operations/training using nonstandard equipment from their own operational commander.

(2) Have been authorized by-name and in writing by CG, MARCORSYSCOM to use specific nonstandard equipment while assigned to or in support of MARCORSYSCOM (IWS/R) for a specified duration and purpose.

c. _Authorized Maintainers_

(1) _Military_. MARCORSYSCOM (IWS/R) is the only authorized Marine Corps owner and maintainer of non-standard parachute equipment. All non-standard parachute equipment owned by MARCORSYSCOM will be packed, maintained and stored in a paraloft by a qualified ram-air parachute rigger with an FAA Senior or Master Parachute Rigger license.

(2) _Civilian_. Approved MARCORSYSCOM civilian contractors and industry-qualified personnel with the above-listed qualifications may conditionally pack and perform maintenance on Marine Corps-owned non-standard parachute equipment. This by-name, written authorization will come from the first Colonel or O-6 in the MARCORSYSCOM (IWS/R) chain of command.

d. _Packing Requirements_. All non-standard parachute equipment will be packed, maintained, and stored in accordance with references (aa) and (ab), and parachute equipment manufacturer's instructions.

e. _RDT&E Authorizations_. As a function of RDT&E, MARCORSYSCOM (IWS/R) is authorized to

(1) Use non-standard parachute equipment on Federal Aviation Administration (FAA)-approved drop zones in accordance with FAA and United States Parachute Association (USPA) rules and regulations.

(2) Deviate from DOD-approved parachute packing requirements in order to develop parachute rigger packing procedures for non-standard equipment.

(3) Use civilian vendors and FAA qualifications as required to develop new approved RAPS capabilities as required.

Chapter 12

Paraloft Requirements

1. <u>General</u>. This chapter provides detailed information on the policy, definitions, authorities, responsibilities, and procedures associated with unit requirements pertaining to maintaining a paraloft facility in support of parachute training.

2. <u>Facility Requirements</u>. Personnel and cargo parachutes and associated airdrop equipment are considered Life Support Equipment and are to be maintained within a facility with strict control. Paraloft facilities will be maintained in accordance with references (aa), (ac), (ae), all applicable equipment technical manuals, and amplifying instructions in this Order.

3. <u>Storage and Security</u>

   a. Stored parachute assemblies that are packed Ready For Issue (RFI) will be stored in a secure manner, inaccessible to unauthorized personnel. This may include approved embark containers.

   b. Paraloft access is to be strictly controlled. Only command-designated personnel are authorized unescorted access to the main paraloft facility and parachute storage room. Undesignated personnel require the escort of a Parachute Rigger (MOS 0451).

   c. Parachutes pending maintenance or re-pack will be maintained separately from parachutes that categorized as RFI. Additionally, parachutes and parachute equipment will be stored and maintained separate from any Helicopter Rope Suspension Equipment.

4. <u>Oxygen-Safe Areas</u>

   a. Oxygen-safe areas will be well ventilated to prevent the dangerous pooling of oxygen. Every attempt will be made to eliminate all potential ignition sources such as grease, oils, static electricity, excessive dust, and sparking outlets at floor level. Doors to oxygen-safe areas will remain open during the transfer of oxygen.

   b. Oxygen storage containers (K-Bottles) will be stored securely to prevent movement and unauthorized access.

5. <u>Lighting</u>. Maintenance and packing areas for life support equipment requires sufficient lighting. Ideal lighting for these functions ranges between 70-140 foot candles per square foot.

6. <u>Drying Towers and Wash Tubs</u>. Parachutes and airdrop equipment will be washed and dried only to prevent malfunction or deterioration. Washtubs are required to wash and rinse this equipment, and circulation of air in the drying towers speeds and facilitates this process.

7. <u>Climate Control</u>

   a. Parachutes and airdrop equipment will be stored in climate controlled environments. Ideal conditions include temperature of 75 degrees Fahrenheit and relative humidity of 60 percent. While temperatures outside the range of 50 to 95 degrees and relative humidity outside of the range of 25 to 80 percent are considered unsafe conditions, temperature deviations from 40 to 120 degrees are authorized for brief durations, but should be avoided whenever possible. Because rapid and extreme changes in temperature can produce condensation, any changes in temperature or humidity should be gradual.

b. Embark containers approved for the secure long term storage of parachutes and airdrop equipment will not be exposed to direct sunlight.

c. Temperature and humidity monitoring systems are required in all parachute storage, packing and maintenance areas, as well as any oxygen-safe areas. Measurements will be recorded and maintained on file per chapter 5 of this Order. Monitoring systems will be centrally located within the designated space for monitoring avoiding exterior walls.

8. Tools. Tools used in the packing of parachutes and maintenance of airdrop equipment will be stored in a designated, secure space. Each paraloft will establish a tool control program to account for and track the use of each parachute packing tool. Tools will be accounted for at the end of each equipment maintenance function and parachute re-pack. Temporary packing pins and other small tools used when packing parachutes will have a yellow or red flag attached of at least eight inches in length.

9. Inspections. The Naval Safety Center (C 44) will inspect paralofts on a regularly scheduled basis and will provide commanders with results and recommendations for improvements and/or corrective actions. In most cases, parachute operations will continue with the implementation of corrective actions to mitigate risk. Repeat discrepancies and trends will be reported to DC, PP&O (POG), DC, I&L (LPC), and COMMARCORSYSCOM (IWS/R) for appropriate action.

Chapter 13

Reporting Requirements

1. General. This chapter provides detailed information on the policy, definitions, authorities, responsibilities, and procedures associated with reporting requirements pertaining to parachute training.

2. Standard Reports. Units and activities responsible for conducting parachute operations will submit the following required reports. Commanders will maintain these reports in accordance with reference (j), SSIC 3500.1.

    a. Joint Airdrop Summary Report (JASR). No later than the 5th calendar day of each month, commanders of Marine Corps units and activities with parachute requirements will submit a JASR (DD 1748-3) covering the previous month to the Naval Safety Center (C 44), USMC Parachute Safety Analyst via official mail, fax or electronically to the addresses below. This reporting requirement is exempt from reports control in accordance with reference (af), Part IV, paragraph 7.h.

        (1) Naval Safety Center (Tactical Operations)
            USMC Parachute Safety Analyst (C 44)
            375 A Street
            Norfolk, VA 23511

        (2) Fax (757) 444-6044, DSN 564-6044

        (3) Safe-code44@navy.mil

    b. Annual Airdrop Roster. No later than 10 January of each calendar year, Naval Safety Center (C 44), USMC Parachute Safety Analyst, will submit a comprehensive roster of all Marine Corps units and activities involved in airdrop operations during the previous calendar year to DC PP&O (POG), DC I&L (LPC), CG MARCORSYSCOM (IWS/R) and MARCOREP Ft. Lee, VA. This reporting requirement is exempt from reports control in accordance with reference (af), Part IV, paragraph 7.h. The purpose of this report is to facilitate HQMC validation of parachute billets, training and equipment requirements for Marine Corps units and activities.

3. Equipment Malfunctions and Incidents. Commanders will report all parachute equipment malfunctions and incidents for both standard and non-standard personnel and cargo airdrop equipment. This reporting requirement is exempt from reports control in accordance with reference (af), Part IV, paragraph 7.e.

    a. Definitions and Examples

        (1) Malfunctions. An equipment malfunction is defined as the failure of the system or piece of equipment to perform as originally designed whether the equipment failed, human error, or emergency procedure was required. This includes, but is not limited to equipment failures resulting in reserve activation, total malfunction, bag lock, broken static line, broken suspension/steering lines, malfunction of automatic opening device, failure of cargo release, or failure of an extraction system.

        (2) Incidents. An incident is defined as anything that occurs during a parachute operation that is considered abnormal. This includes, but is limited to parachutist activation of his reserve for any reason, activation

of automatic opening devices for any reason, injured parachutists, mid-air entanglements, towed parachutist, jumpers/equipment landing off of the drop zone involving injury or significant damage to equipment, tree or wire landings, and premature pilot chute activation.

b. Responsibility. While the responsibility to report all malfunctions and incidents ultimately rests with the unit commander or officer-in-charge, timely compliance with report requirements is a shared duty between the malfunction officer, jumpmasters, safeties, and drop zone safety officer for the specific parachute operation, as well as the unit parachute safety officer and paraloft chief.

c. Method

(1) Units will report airdrop malfunctions and incidents to the Naval Safety Center after completing the Web Enabled Safety System (WESS) Report Format located at www.safetycenter.navy.mil/ashore/parachuting/default.htm by entering the completed report in the WESS Mishap/Hazard reporting System.

(2) Units without access to or permissions in WESS may submit reports to the Naval Safety Center (C 44), USMC Parachute Safety Analyst via official mail, fax or electronically to the addresses below:

(a) Naval Safety Center (Tactical Operations)
USMC Parachute Safety Analyst (C 44)
375 A Street
Norfolk, VA 23511

(b) Fax (757) 444-6044, DSN 564-6044

(c) Safe-code44@navy.mil

(3) The Naval Safety Center (C 44) will provide the U.S. Army Quartermaster School with a consolidated USMC report in conjunction with the U.S. Army Malfunction Review Board.

d. Accidents Involving Injury or Death. In addition to requirements outlined in reference (h), official Naval Message notification of parachuting malfunctions and incidents resulting in injury or death will be submitted within 24 hours of the incident by the individual's parent command to each of the plain language address designators (PLADs) below.

(1) CMC WASHINGTON DC PPO POG.

(2) CMC WASHINGTON DC L LPC.

(3) CMC WASHINGTON DC MRA MR MRC.

(4) CG MARCORSYSCOM IWS.

(5) COMNAVSAFECEN.

e. Suspected Malfunction of Equipment. In addition to requirements outlined in reference (h), Naval Message notification of suspected malfunction of parachute equipment will be submitted within 12 hours of the malfunction via the chain of command to each of the PLADs below. In the event that Naval Message services are unavailable, a telephonic report can be submitted as a last resort.

(1) CMC WASHINGTON DC PPO POG.

(2) CMC WASHINGTON DC L LPC.

(3) CMC WASHINGTON DC SD.

(4) CG MARCORSYSCOM IWS.

(5) CG MARCORSYSCOM MC2I.

(6) COMNAVSAFECEN.

(7) MARCOREP FT LEE VA.

Enclosure (1)

www.ingramcontent.com/pod-product-compliance
Lightning Source LLC
Chambersburg PA
CBHW080540290526
45790CB00006B/2492